Original title:
The Fox's Echo

Copyright © 2024 Swan Charm
All rights reserved.

Author: Kätriin Kaldaru
ISBN HARDBACK: 978-9908-1-0169-9
ISBN PAPERBACK: 978-9908-1-0170-5
ISBN EBOOK: 978-9908-1-0171-2

Shadows at the Edge of Day

As sunlight fades, the shadows grow,
A dance of colors, a soft, warm glow.
Laughter echoes through the air,
Joyful spirits everywhere.

Beneath the trees, we gather near,
Sharing stories, drinks, and cheer.
The day slips slowly into night,
Hearts are full, the mood is bright.

Fireflies flicker, a magical sight,
Stars begin to twinkle alight.
In this moment, time stands still,
A perfect night, a dream fulfilled.

So let us savor every breeze,
With open hearts, we find our ease.
In shadows long, our spirits play,
Embracing life at end of day.

Dreaming Beneath the Starlit Canopy

Beneath the stars, we spread a quilt,
In moonlit glow, a dream is built.
Soft whispers float on gentle sighs,
As constellations light the skies.

Laughter sparkles like the night,
With every joke, we feel the light.
The universe, our cosmic friend,
Ideas flow, and hearts extend.

Sipping nectar from the vine,
Each moment tastes like sweet divine.
The world outside fades far away,
In starlit dreams, we long to stay.

Together here, our souls align,
In this embrace, we feel so fine.
Beneath the starlit canopy wide,
In dreams we dance, with love as guide.

Tread Quietly in the Gloaming

As daylight wanes, the colors shift,
In gloaming light, we find the gift.
The air is sweet with secrets shared,
In whispered tones, we show we cared.

Step lightly on the twilight path,
Fleeting moments, a gentle laugh.
The world grows still, a hush descends,
With open hearts, our joy transcends.

Golden hues paint the lingering sky,
We dance beneath, let worries fly.
In shadowed corners, memories bloom,
Together here, we cast out gloom.

So tread with care, yet let hearts sing,
In this brief pause, let freedom spring.
The night awaits with open arms,
In gloaming's glow, we find our charms.

Twilight's Enigmatic Dance

As twilight falls, the world transforms,
A dreamy haze in myriad forms.
Colors swirl in a mystic trance,
We find our rhythm in this dance.

The sky ablaze with hues divine,
In every heartbeat, we intertwine.
With laughter echoing, spirits high,
We chase the stars, let worries fly.

Mysterious whispers on the breeze,
In twilight's glow, the heart's at ease.
Each fleeting moment, a jewel rare,
A tapestry woven with love and care.

So hold my hand, let's twirl away,
In this enchanting, bright ballet.
With every step, the night enhances,
Come lose yourself in twilight's dances.

Specters of the Silent Grove

In the grove where shadows dance,
Laughter twinkles, a fleeting glance.
Banners wave on the gentle breeze,
Echoes of joy come with such ease.

Whispers linger, stories unfold,
A tapestry of wonders told.
Moonlight glimmers on leaves so bright,
Enchanted realms in the soft night.

Rapture of the Night's Lore

Stars above in a grand array,
Celebrate this vibrant play.
Luminous dreams ignite the sky,
As night unfolds with a tender sigh.

Melodies weave through the silken air,
Carried lightly without a care.
Every heartbeat sings with glee,
In the rapture of night's decree.

Whispers of the Whimsical Trail

Take a step on the path so bright,
Where magic brews in the pale moonlight.
Every corner holds a surprise,
With glittering joy that never dies.

Frolicsome winds in the trees do play,
As laughter echoes along the way.
Dancing spirits in garments spun,
Whispers of glee till the night is done.

Dusk's Playful Deceiver

At dusk, the world wears a playful hue,
Painting dreams in shades anew.
Twilight swirls with giddy delight,
Inviting all to celebrate the night.

In the glow of lanterns spun,
The festivities have just begun.
Beneath the stars, with hearts so bold,
Dances unfold, a tale retold.

Whispers in the Thicket

Laughter rings where shadows play,
Brighting leaves on a vibrant day.
Tiny lights in the twilight glow,
Whispers dance where the breezes flow.

Children chase in a merry spree,
Gleeful voices as sweet as can be.
Baskets filled with delights abound,
Joyful moments in every sound.

Picnic spreads on a checkered cloth,
Under the branches, no way to sloth.
Songs are sung with spirits so high,
In this thicket, the world passes by.

As stars peek out, the night ignites,
With tales told soft, in soft twilight's sights.
Magic woven in the silk of the air,
Festive whispers, beyond compare.

Shadows of the Cunning

In moonlit glades, the mischief stirs,
With foxes prancing as night prefers.
Cunning eyes watch from oak's embrace,
Tricks and laughter, a playful chase.

Whiskers twitching, a riddle to solve,
Puzzles abound, as all evolve.
With every dart, a cheer breaks free,
In shadows long, where joys decree.

Glimmers of fur, soft in the dark,
Promises whispered, each secret spark.
Wily hearts in a woodland dance,
Adventures bloom with every chance.

So raise a toast to the cunning crew,
Under the stars, dreams come true.
In laughter's glow, no worries remain,
In shadows we dance, in joy unchained.

Echoes of the Woodland

Upon the trail where echoes ring,
Voices mingle like birds in spring.
A tapestry of sound and sight,
In woodland's heart, pure delight.

Rustling leaves in a gentle breeze,
Nature's concert, bringing peace.
Each note a heartbeat, rhythmic and clear,
Gathering all who wander near.

Under the canopy's lush embrace,
Community thrives in this sacred space.
Hand in hand, we share our tales,
In echoes alive, joy never fails.

As day fades soft into the night,
Starlit dreams take glorious flight.
With every flicker, hopes intertwine,
In woodland's echo, our spirits shine.

Furtive Footsteps at Dusk

As day surrenders to evening's glow,
Furtive footsteps start to flow.
Mysteries linger in twilight's charm,
Creeping softly, with calm arm.

Shadowed paths that curious roam,
Heartbeats quicken, feelings of home.
The rustle of grass, a melody pure,
In twilight's magic, we all endure.

With whispers low, and giggles bright,
Secrets shared beneath soft light.
Nimble spirits in a gentle stack,
At dusk we gather, no looking back.

The world unfolds in colors warm,
Each quiet step brings forth the charm.
In furtive footsteps, we unite,
The joy of dusk, our hearts ignite.

Chasing Becalmed Dreams

In twilight's embrace, laughter flows,
Joy dances lightly, as the evening glows.
With whispers of stars in the gentle night,
We chase the calm dreams, taking flight.

Balloons in the air, colors afloat,
We share the sweet moments, hearts that gloat.
Echoes of friendship, warm and bright,
As we weave our stories, under the light.

Flickers in Autumn's Veil

Leaves twirl like dancers, in scarlet and gold,
Each gust of the breeze, a tale to be told.
Pumpkins are smiling, candles aglow,
Festive delights, in the evening's flow.

Gathered together, warmth fills the air,
Laughter and music, sweet moments we share.
Flickers of joy in the crisp autumn chill,
Hearts intertwined, as we savor the thrill.

Tangles of Elusive Pursuit

Chasing the echoes of laughter's delight,
We dance through the shadows, embracing the night.
With fireflies blinking, like wishes come true,
We skip through the meadows, just me and you.

The thrill of the chase, a game to unfold,
Tangles of dreams, like ribbons of gold.
As stars twinkle brightly, we lose track of time,
In pursuit of joy, a whimsical rhyme.

Enigmas in the Distant Brush

Whispers of secrets swirl in the air,
Under the moonlight, we wander without care.
The night is alive, with music and cheer,
Enigmas surround us, as we draw near.

With lanterns aglow, we traverse the path,
In search of the wonders that spark our own laugh.
Each step a discovery, each moment a bliss,
In the festive night's cradle, we find our sweet kiss.

Specters of the Silent Prowl

Beneath the stars, the whispers play,
Gleaming lights in night's ballet.
Veils of joy dance in the air,
Cloaked in laughter, free from care.

Sparkling eyes and hidden smiles,
Echoes of joy stretch for miles.
In shadows deep, the secrets twirl,
As festive spirits freely whirl.

Traces of the Wandering Spirit

Through emerald paths where fairies tread,
A melody sparks, dances widespread.
Whistling winds like soft accord,
Call forth dreams, in bliss, restored.

Curtains of dusk drape the glade,
While laughter's song their shadows aid.
Nimble steps, the spirits sway,
In celebration, night turns to day.

Lore of the Listless Woods

In whispering leaves, stories unfold,
Of radiant days and nights of gold.
Cascades of joy in rustling breeze,
Inviting hearts with gentle tease.

Echoes of laughter, twinkling spheres,
Chasing away all hidden fears.
Among the trees, friendships spark,
In the glow of the moon's soft arc.

Secrets in the Moonshine

In moonlit glow, the secrets gleam,
Woven in whispers, a festive dream.
Twilight calls with a playful sigh,
Drawing close the spirits nigh.

With each heartbeat, the night ignites,
Carries forth resplendent sights.
Under silvery blankets, we find,
The magic of the heart, intertwined.

Reflections of a Wily Spirit

In the twilight glow, laughter rings,
Whispers of joy on ephemeral wings.
Glints of mischief in the air,
A playful dance, without a care.

Mirthful echoes under the moon,
The night sings a vibrant tune.
Shadows twirl, shadows weave,
In this merry night, we believe.

Bright colors clash, hearts beat fast,
Each moment a treasure, never to last.
With spirits high, we toast and cheer,
Embracing the magic, drawing near.

As dawn approaches, we'll reminisce,
Holding tight to the night's bliss.
Reflections in laughter, so grand,
Bonded forever, heart in hand.

Silhouettes in the Glade

Under the boughs, a secret dance,
Silhouettes move in a twilight trance.
Laughter mingles with the breeze,
In this glade, we find our ease.

Crickets chirp their sweet refrain,
As candles flicker, holding flame.
A gathering of souls, warm and bright,
Painting the canvas of the night.

Joyful cheers rise up high,
Stars join in from the sky.
With every step, with every sway,
We celebrate life in vibrant array.

Moments captured, hearts entwined,
In this glade, our dreams aligned.
Together we share this radiant space,
Embracing the night, love's embrace.

Prowl of the Enigmatic

Under the stars, the shadows play,
An enigmatic night, let's drift away.
Secrets whispered, tales unfold,
Adventures await, daring and bold.

In the moonlight's soft caress,
We dance through woods, hearts confess.
Mysterious paths and hidden sights,
Illuminated by the dreamy lights.

With every rustle, our spirits lift,
The forest hums, a magical gift.
The unknown lingers, teasing, bright,
Guided by stars, we spark the night.

In the embrace of shadows deep,
We find the promises that we keep.
Together we roam, nowhere to hide,
In the prowl of the night, side by side.

Shivers in the Shade

Beneath the boughs where whispers play,
The breeze feels cool, a sweet bouquet.
Giggling voices fill the air,
With every glance, magic is there.

Dappled sunlight breaks through the leaves,
Enticing shivers, joy that weaves.
A banquet laid with colors bright,
Celebrations dance in the fading light.

With every sip, with every bite,
Our laughter soars, pure delight.
Stories shared, memories made,
In the warmth of friendship, fears allayed.

As shadows stretch and day declines,
We cherish the moments, the love that shines.
Together we bask in this gentle shade,
Forever with joy, our hearts serenade.

Whirl of the Whispering Winds

In the breeze, laughter twirls,
Colors dance, and joy unfurls.
Balloons rise to the azure sky,
As whispers of cheer softly sigh.

Sparkling lights wink through the trees,
Echoing dreams in a playful tease.
Children giggle, hearts alive,
In this moment, we all thrive.

Candles flicker, stories unfold,
In the warmth, our memories hold.
Everyone gathers, hand in hand,
Together we weave, this joyful strand.

Under the stars, the night glows bright,
With every moment, pure delight.
The world is alive, laughter rings,
In the whirl of the whispering winds.

Enchanter of Silent Ferns

In the glade where shadows play,
Ferns weave secrets in their sway.
Crickets chirp a soft refrain,
While moonlight dances on the lane.

Flowers bloom with radiant grace,
Adding magic to the space.
Whispers linger in the air,
As night unveils her treasures rare.

A gentle breeze, a tender sigh,
Stars emerge in the velvet sky.
Laughter weaves through the night air,
Casting spells for all who dare.

In the stillness, joy will reign,
Embracing hearts without a chain.
Together we sing, take our turn,
With the enchanter of silent ferns.

Twilight's Trickster

As twilight falls, the world transforms,
In shades of purple, beauty warms.
The horizon glows with playful hues,
A canvas rich, with life anew.

Laughter spills from every nook,
In shadowed paths where we once took.
The fireflies dance, a twinkling show,
Guiding our steps, where dreams will flow.

With every breeze, a secret shared,
In whispered tales, love is declared.
Masquerades of joy unfold,
As twilight's trickster weaves the gold.

Voices echo, sweet and clear,
Calling us close, casting off fear.
With every heartbeat, the night sings,
A symphony of all good things.

Murmurs from the Mysterious

In the hush of the twilight mist,
Murmurs rise, a gentle twist.
Secrets held in the cozy dark,
Where shadows flicker, and dreams spark.

The forest hums a melodious tune,
Under silver smiles of the moon.
Each rustle and sigh beckons the bold,
To unfold stories waiting to be told.

A twinkle of laughter, echoes sway,
As magic dances in bright array.
Together, we weave a tale divine,
In the whispers of the night, we shine.

Through the mystery, we find our way,
Hand in hand, come what may.
With every murmur, we draw near,
In this festive night, we have no fear.

Rustle of the Hidden Ones

Beneath the stars, secrets dance,
Laughter echoes, a merry prance.
In twilight's glow, spirits rise,
A festival bright, under moonlit skies.

Leaves shimmer softly, winds caress,
Joyful hearts in a wild press.
From shadows leap, life takes flight,
With every whisper, a spark of light.

The hidden ones join in the song,
Where friendship and spirit both belong.
Bubbling laughter, a bubbling brook,
In every corner, a magic nook.

As night unfolds, the stories blend,
In festive cheer, the spirits send.
Under the arch of the ancient trees,
The rustle of joy floats in the breeze.

Chasing Moonlit Reflections

Dancing shadows on the lake,
Moonlit paths, a night to awake.
Whispers shared with gentle gleam,
In the night's embrace, we dream.

Reflections shimmer, stars align,
Hearts entwine with a sip of wine.
Echoes of laughter gently flare,
Under the silvered, starlit air.

A night where wishes glide and sway,
Each moment precious, none would stray.
Chasing dreams on a fleeting beam,
As life flows softly like a dream.

Laughter weaves through the quiet night,
In every corner, festive delight.
With every spark that winks and glows,
Chasing moonlit dreams, the spirit grows.

Whispers from the Underbrush

In the heath, where shadows dwell,
Come the whispers, a secret spell.
Crickets sing in the evening shade,
Festive murmurs serenely played.

The rustling grass, a melody sweet,
Nature's chorus, a rhythmic beat.
Under the firs, life hums and plays,
Inviting joy in secret ways.

Flickering fireflies, night's bright crown,
Guide the wanderers through the town.
With hearts aglow and spirits high,
In the underbrush, we laugh and sigh.

Beneath the glow of a silver moon,
The world transforms to a joyful tune.
Whispers calling, inviting all,
To join the dance at nature's ball.

The Vanished Shade

In twilight's embrace, the shadows blend,
A festive call where old tales send.
The vanished shade, a fleeting glance,
In every heart, a hidden dance.

Among the flowers, spirits twine,
Life's sweet nectar, rich as wine.
Echoes of laughter fill the air,
In the whispering woods, joy to share.

A flick of color, a glimpse so rare,
The vanished shade leads hearts to dare.
Each corner holds a story bright,
In the embrace of the gentle night.

As stories fade and shadows play,
In every moment, the bright array.
The vanished shade, with a gentle grace,
Calls forth the joy we all embrace.

Wandering Glances at Dusk

As the sun dips low and shadows blend,
Laughter echoes, a joyful trend.
Colors swirl in the evening's grace,
Wandering hearts in a vibrant embrace.

Bubbles burst in the soft twilight,
Glimmers of joy, a wondrous sight.
Stars waltz out, a shimmering parade,
Underneath the dusk, memories cascade.

Whispers float through the gathering breeze,
With every smile, the world feels at ease.
Children chase dreams where fireflies gleam,
In this festive moment, life's a dream.

Time slips away, yet joy stays still,
Each glance shared, a heart to fill.
In the dusk, we find our light,
Together we dance into the night.

Hues of the Night's Charade

Under the veil of a velvety sky,
Colors entwine as the night flits by.
Candles flicker with secrets to tell,
In this vibrant place where shadows dwell.

Faces glow with a warm, soft sheen,
Laughter erupts, the air feels serene.
A tapestry woven with joy's own thread,
In the heart of the night, our dreams are spread.

Jazz notes ripple, the rhythm ignites,
With every beat, our spirit takes flight.
Twirling with joy, we sway in delight,
In hues of the night, everything feels right.

So let us wander through this lively charade,
Where every moment is joyfully played.
With friends surrounding, let's share the cheer,
Under the stars, all worries disappear.

Glistening Fables of the Furtive

In the corners where the warm lights glow,
Glistening stories begin to flow.
Each whispered tale, a magic thread,
Of laughter and love that's softly spread.

Tiny sparks dance in the night's embrace,
Furtive glances with a playful grace.
Unfolding chapters of joy and delight,
Under the stars, our hearts take flight.

Happiness lingers like the sweet scent of cake,
As smiles and stories intertwine and awake.
Every corner holds a new surprise,
In this night of wonder, the spirit flies.

So raise a toast to the magic we weave,
Each fable sparkling, in dreams we believe.
Glistening moments blend into one,
Under this night, we've only begun.

Intricacies of the Silent Dance

Beneath a canopy of twinkling lights,
We sway gently, lost in delights.
The world hushes, and time drifts away,
In the intricate waltz, we find our play.

Every heartbeat dances to a soft tune,
With whispers of joy and the crescent moon.
Our shadows mingle in a tender embrace,
As we move together, a passionate chase.

The air is thick with laughter's sweet song,
In this silent dance, we all belong.
Every look shared ignites the flame,
In the festival's spirit, we're never the same.

So let the rhythm paint our night bright,
With intricacies woven in starlit light.
Together, we dance through laughter and cheer,
In this joyous moment, forever near.

Lament of the Lost Trails

In the gold of the fading light,
Whispers of paths once bright.
Echoes of laughter that filled the air,
Now just memories, scattered everywhere.

Underneath the twilight's glow,
Footsteps linger, moving slow.
Journey's end, a tale untold,
Dreams of adventure, now turned cold.

Echoes of Stealthy Steps

In shadows deep, where silence reigns,
Where secrets hide, the heart still pains.
Softly moving like whispered winds,
The night conceals what darkness lends.

With every pause, the world at bay,
Stealthy echoes weave their play.
The thrill of night, a dance in time,
Hidden paths, a secret rhyme.

Dance of the Autumn Leaves

Rustling colors paint the ground,
As autumn's breath swirls all around.
Leaves flutter like whispers of day,
In nature's waltz, they gently sway.

Golden hues and crimson shades,
In the breeze, their beauty fades.
The world transforms, a canvas bright,
In the heart of fall, pure delight.

The Woodland's Silent Watcher

Amidst the trees, tall and grand,
A guardian stands, silent and planned.
With branches wide, it spreads its grace,
A keeper of secrets in this sacred space.

Whispering winds tell tales of old,
Of fleeting moments, brave and bold.
In quietude, it holds the key,
To memories cherished, wild and free.

Sly Shadows Beneath the Stars

In twilight's glow, the laughter flows,
Dancing shadows, where the moonlight knows.
Whispers of joy in the night so sweet,
Footsteps echo, where friends greet.

Lanterns flicker in the gentle breeze,
As hearts unite beneath the trees.
A tapestry woven with stories shared,
In every glance, love is declared.

Stars above, like diamonds bright,
Guide our dreams on this festive night.
With every twirl and every cheer,
We celebrate each moment here.

The world transforms in this cosmic dance,
As souls entwine in a merry trance.
Beneath the stars, our spirits soar,
In sly shadows, we crave for more.

Nightfall's Illusions

As day retreats, the night awakes,
A stage is set for the joy it makes.
Fireflies shimmer in the cool night air,
Casting illusions, enchanting and rare.

The laughter rises, a magical song,
Carried by breezes, where we belong.
Under starlit skies, our tales unfold,
In nightfall's embrace, warm and bold.

With every star, a wish we send,
Dreams intertwine, as moments blend.
The heartbeat of night, a rhythm so true,
In this festive dance, it's me and you.

From dusk till dawn, let spirits collide,
In revelry's clutch, together we glide.
Nightfall's illusions, like rivers they flow,
Guiding our hearts through the inky glow.

Tales of the Roaming Spirit

In moonlit meadows, stories unfold,
Tales of the roaming spirit, bold.
With every step, history sings,
Echoes of laughter on gossamer wings.

The winds carry whispers of ages past,
In every shadow, memories cast.
Under the stars, we wander free,
As spirits dance in wild jubilee.

Around the fire, stories ignite,
With every flicker, we embrace the night.
Laughter and joy paint the air,
In this vibrant realm, we choose to share.

From hearts intertwined, a festive tide,
Together we roam, side by side.
Tales of our journey, forever to keep,
In the spirit's embrace, we dare to leap.

Footprints in the Fog

Through silver mist, we leave our trace,
Footprints in the fog, a fleeting space.
With every step, our laughter blends,
In the heart of night, where magic sends.

Ghostly whispers in the shroud of night,
Guide our journey with soft delight.
As lanterns glow like stars we chase,
The festive spirit fills the place.

Each twinkle spark, a memory earned,
In the foggy glow, our passions burned.
We weave through shadows, heartbeats align,
In a realm of wonder, tales intertwine.

As dawn approaches, our footprints fade,
Yet the night's embrace, we won't evade.
For every moment was rich and bright,
In the echoes of joy, we found our light.

Shadows of the Clever Spirit

In the evening's gentle glow,
Laughter dances, spirits flow.
With twinkling lights and songs so bright,
The shadows leap in sheer delight.

Beneath the stars, the tales unfold,
Whispers shared, secrets told.
In the air, a magic sound,
As joy and wonder swirl around.

In every corner, smiles ignite,
Celebrations through the night.
Champagne bubbles, cheers resound,
In shadows, clever spirits found.

So let us move and let us sway,
In this festive, bright ballet.
With harmony, we raise a cheer,
For every heart and soul is dear.

Enigmatic Serenade in the Pines

Among the pines, a melody plays,
Echoing through those joyful days.
A serenade to make us dance,
In this moment, we find our chance.

With firelight flickering in the dark,
Stories shared, leaving a spark.
The crisp air fills with laughter's song,
In this place, we all belong.

Moonlit whispers caress the leaves,
While everyone around believes.
In nature's arms, we sway and sigh,
As magic dances through the sky.

Embrace the night, let worries cease,
For joy and love grant us peace.
In the pines, forever near,
The enigmatic spirit draws us here.

Flicker of the Furtive

A flicker here, a glimmer there,
Whispers floating in cool air.
In shadows cast by lantern's light,
The furtive sparkle shines so bright.

As laughter spills, the secrets blend,
With chances taken, rules to bend.
In festive cheer, we rise and twirl,
In this enchanted, joyous whirl.

Mirth and mischief share the night,
With every flicker, hearts take flight.
As sparklers glow, the memories gleam,
In this moment, we chase a dream.

With every heart, the rhythm sways,
In a dance that lasts for days.
A furtive glimpse, a tale of glow,
As we celebrate what we know.

Riddles of the Rustic Realm

In the rustic realm where laughter grows,
Riddles echo as twilight glows.
With every cheer, a story's spun,
In the dance of hearts, we all are one.

Under the leaves, the lanterns sway,
Their gentle light leads the way.
With cups raised high and voices clear,
In unity, we cast out fear.

Amidst the whispers, futures tread,
With every riddle, dreams are fed.
In friendly jest, all troubles fade,
In this rustic realm, love is laid.

So feel the heartbeat of this night,
With every face, a radiant light.
Together here, we forge the bond,
In riddles woven, we respond.

Flickers of Illusive Light

In the twilight's embrace, bright hues glow,
Dancing shadows whisper with the soft breeze,
Laughter erupts like the bubbles that flow,
As hearts intertwine 'neath the moonlit trees.

Sparkling spirits rise from the earth's deep core,
With every flicker, joy paints the night air,
Chasing the darkness, inviting much more,
A symphony woven with love and with care.

Glimmers of dreams float like colors on high,
The warmth of togetherness lights up the face,
Wishes take flight, riding on hope's sweet sigh,
Embracing the magic, we dance, we race.

So let the night sing with its enchanting charms,
Where moments are cherished, and spirits are bright,
In this space of wonder, where love always warms,
We dazzle like stars in this flickering light.

Secrets in the Starlit Grove

Beneath the sky's canvas, secrets unfold,
In the starlit grove where the fireflies twirl,
Whispers of laughter and stories retold,
Embrace the enchantment in every soft swirl.

The moon, a guardian, watches the play,
While shadows dance lightly on soft, verdant ground,
With every heartbeat, joy finds its way,
In the symphony of night, all worries unbound.

Crickets are singing their magical tune,
As friendship blooms brightly, like flowers in spring,
In the glow of the stars, hearts drift and swoon,
Every laughter a melody, happily ringing.

So gather your dreams in this twilight's hold,
Feel the warmth of connection in briefest of nights,
In the starlit grove, our stories are bold,
Illuminated secrets, pure festive delights.

Enigma of the Dusky Woods

In the dusky woods, where shadows play tricks,
A mystery beckons from branches and leaves,
With laughter that dances, it twirls and it flips,
While light flickers softly, as night softly weaves.

Whispers of twilight call forth the divine,
From hidden nooks where the wild roses bloom,
As fireflies gather in elegant lines,
Wearing the dusk like a silken costume.

The air is alive with the sound of pure glee,
Voices adorned in the warmth of the night,
Bound together, like roots of a tree,
We carry the joy, as we bask in the light.

So join the enigma, let laughter ignite,
In the dusky woods, where wonders unite,
With every heart shared, and dreams taking flight,
A festive delight, shining ever so bright.

The Vagabond's Howl

In the still of the night, a howl takes its turn,
From a vagabond's heart, wild stories are spun,
Echoes of laughter like flames that will burn,
In the revelry deep where the magic's begun.

With a wink and a smile, the night cracks awake,
Underneath silver skies, we gather and roam,
In search of bright treasures, that dreams often make,
Exploring the corners, we sculpt our own home.

Like leaves in the wind, we swirl and we sway,
With each breath infused with a spirit so free,
The howl of the vagabond leads us away,
To dance in the starlight, just you, me, and we.

So raise up your glass to the night's joyful call,
To the vagabond howl that inspires the bold,
In every heartbeat, we flourish, we fall,
Festive, untamed, where our stories unfold.

Rhythms of the Wild Heart

In the forest, drums beat loud,
Dancing shadows sway and bow.
Stars above wear crowns of light,
Celebrate the joyful night.

Laughter echoes through the trees,
A melody carried by the breeze.
Hearts unite in vibrant cheer,
As nature sings for all to hear.

Colors sparkle, joy takes flight,
Every soul ignites the night.
Whispers blend in sweet embrace,
In this wild, enchanted space.

Together we rejoice and play,
Merriment to guide our way.
Each heartbeat marks a tune of grace,
As we dance in Nature's embrace.

The Silent Trickster

Under the moon, a sly surprise,
A fleeting glance, mischief in disguise.
Silent shadows weave their art,
With playful tricks that tug the heart.

Whispers float on winds so light,
Joyful laughter fills the night.
Paths unfold in twinkling light,
As secrets dance beyond our sight.

Chasing dreams through twilight's glow,
Laughter hides where no one goes.
In the stillness, joy takes flight,
In this playful, silent night.

The trickster grins, a wink to share,
With every soul who dares to care.
In this realm of joyous play,
Come, join the dance of night and day.

Whispers of the Woodland

Beneath the boughs, the stories weave,
In every rustle, magic leaves.
The woodland breathes a song so sweet,
With every heartbeat, life's complete.

Frolicsome spirits charm the air,
With playful tricks beyond compare.
Joyful gatherings in leafy glades,
Memories linger in dappled shades.

A tapestry of colors bright,
Crafted in the soft moonlight.
Whispers echo, secrets sway,
As night reveals a grand ballet.

Together we in harmony sing,
To the magic each moment brings.
The woodland calls, come take part,
In the dance of the wild heart.

Secrets in the Shadows

In the hush where shadows dwell,
Mysteries weave a silent spell.
A flicker of light, a whispered laugh,
Life in secret; a hidden path.

With every corner, tales unfold,
Of joy and wonder yet untold.
In twilight's embrace, the heart ignites,
A festive spirit dances through nights.

Veils of night, where laughter hides,
Invite us to explore the sides.
A treasure trove of hidden glows,
In secret realms where magic flows.

We gather close, in shadows play,
As the night transforms our way.
In these secrets, hearts align,
Under the stars, where love will shine.

Mystique of the Untamed Path

Beneath a sky of twinkling stars,
Dancing lights lead us afar.
Laughter echoes through the trees,
Nature hums in joyful breeze.

Footprints trace a playful dance,
Every shadow sparks romance.
Wildflowers bloom, colors bright,
Together, we embrace the night.

Whispers ride on fragrant air,
Harmonies of life we share.
A world alive with pure delight,
At every turn, a new ignite.

Through secret paths, our spirits soar,
In this embrace, forevermore.
Let the wildness intertwine,
As we trace this magic line.

Phantoms of the Twilight Trail

A twilight glow on dusky ground,
With serenades of night profound.
Mysterious echoes fill the air,
As whispers dance without a care.

Phantoms drift through silver glow,
Chasing dreams where shadows flow.
The moon above, a guiding sage,
Illuminates this vibrant stage.

With every turn, new wonders tease,
Enchanting depths the heart can seize.
In this realm of magic we find,
The essence of the night entwined.

Let joy resound as stars ignite,
And fairy tales come into sight.
The trail unfolds with joyous cheer,
Each phantom brings the heart near.

Whispers of the Moonlit Hunt

In silver shades where shadows blend,
A world awakens, dreams transcend.
The hunt begins with laughter's sound,
Underneath the moonlit ground.

Soft footsteps tread on fragrant leaves,
As night unveils what daylight weaves.
With every rustle, spirits rise,
Reveling in the starlit skies.

Each whisper fuels the thrill inside,
A joyful chase, our hearts collide.
In the dance of night, we roam free,
Together, wild as we can be.

With treasures found in every glance,
The moon invites us to our dance.
In this magic, we take flight,
With whispers shared in another light.

Flickers in the Foliage

Amidst the leaves, soft lights abound,
Flickers of joy in every sound.
The woodland hums, a festive cheer,
As nature's wonders draw us near.

Tiny glows like stars at play,
Bring life to shadows on display.
We gather round with hearts aglow,
In this embrace, the spirits grow.

Songs of laughter dance like streams,
Unveiling all our wildest dreams.
Each glimmer guides us through the night,
With flickers leading, pure delight.

United here, we hold the light,
In foliage dressed, our souls take flight.
For in this place of gentle ease,
We find the wonders that please.

Echoes of the Night Prowler

Under a sky of velvet blue,
Whispers float with the evening dew.
Laughter dances in the cool night air,
Radiant stars become our fare.

With shadows weaving a mental thread,
Dreams awaken, adventures spread.
The moonlight twinkles on faces bright,
Guardians of joy in the heart of night.

The night owl calls, a merry tune,
While fireflies play 'neath the glowing moon.
Every echo tells a story sweet,
Join the revelry, feel the beat.

Chasing giggles through the gentle dark,
With each fleeting moment, we leave our mark.
In the revels of this starry show,
Together we shine, together we glow.

Lore of the Luminous Path

Dancing lanterns line the street,
With every flicker, joy we meet.
Songs of old weave through the night,
Stars above twinkle with delight.

Underneath the old oak tree,
Whispers of the past call to me.
Tales of love and laughter thrive,
On this path where memories dive.

With friends gathered close in cheer,
Echoes of laughter ring so clear.
Each footstep taken, a heartbeat strong,
In this luminous path, we all belong.

Night unfolds, a canvas bright,
In the warmth of friendship's light.
Here we dance, here we sing,
Life's rich tapestry weaves everything.

Wily Reflections at Dusk

At dusk the world feels alive,
Colors mingle, dreams revive.
Shadows stretch and stories grow,
In the twilight, magic flows.

A breeze carries laughter near,
Soft whispers only friends can hear.
Stars blink gently, awaiting night,
While fireflies flirt, a dazzling sight.

With each sunset, wonders unfold,
Moments cherished, tales retold.
In wily reflections, we find our place,
Dancing shadows in time's embrace.

The warmth of hearts in the fading light,
Gather 'round, share your delight.
As dusk prepares to greet the stars,
We celebrate who we are.

Chasing Autumn's Tracks

Golden leaves adorn the ground,
Crisp air fills the world around.
Festive spirits bloom and dance,
In every twirl, there's a chance.

Painted skies in twilight's glow,
Harvest moons put on a show.
Laughter echoes through the trees,
Tales of joy ride on the breeze.

Candied apples and warm delights,
Friends gather for cozy nights.
As pumpkins grin with all their might,
We chase the tracks of autumn's light.

In every step, a memory brews,
A celebration in rich autumn hues.
Gather close, feel the embrace,
In this festive, joyful place.

Secrets Beneath the Moonlight

Whispers ride on silver beams,
As secrets flow in vibrant streams.
Laughter sparkles like the stars,
In the night's embrace, we are ours.

Dancing shadows, soft and bright,
Flicker gently in soft light.
Magic weaves through heart and hand,
In this moment, we will stand.

With every smile, the night will sway,
Leading us in a joyous ballet.
Beneath the canopy so wide,
We share our dreams, with hearts as guide.

Let's chase the dawn, our spirits free,
In this realm, just you and me.
With every secret held so tight,
We'll carry joy past morning light.

The Trickster's Serenade

A jester's laugh fills up the air,
With every twist, we shed our care.
Bright colors swirl, a lively sight,
As night cascades with sheer delight.

Echoes of mischief, sweet and bold,
In every tale that's newly told.
Circles dance beneath the trees,
Where laughter carries on the breeze.

Trickster's heart, so full of glee,
Inviting all to join the spree.
Chasing shadows, weaving dreams,
In the dark, we find our themes.

With a wink and a playful tune,
We celebrate beneath the moon.
In this dance, we find our place,
Embracing joy, a warm embrace.

Murmurs of the Forest Floor

Underneath the ancient trees,
Soft whispers float upon the breeze.
Nature's secrets, hushed and low,
In twilight's grasp, they ebb and flow.

With every leaf, a tale is spun,
Of joyous times, of laughter, fun.
Rustling underfoot, we tread light,
In harmony with the starry night.

Fireflies blink like distant stars,
Lighting up our playful scars.
As the night unfolds its charms,
We gather close, in nature's arms.

Murmurs sing from roots and stone,
A sacred rhythm, all our own.
Surrounded by the earth's embrace,
Together, we find our joyous space.

A Dance with the Night Wind

The night wind calls with a gentle sigh,
A silent whisper weaved in the sky.
With open arms, we'll take our flight,
In rhythm with the stars so bright.

Moonlight glimmers on the plain,
As we twirl and spin, free from pain.
Each step we take, the world ignites,
In this dance, our heart delites.

Laughter floats on the midnight air,
As dreams collide without a care.
In nature's symphony, we are one,
Beneath the sky, our hearts outrun.

With every breeze, our spirits soar,
A dance of life forevermore.
In this festive night, let's begin,
A celebration, where hearts are kin.

Tales of the Cunning Hunter

In the glades where laughter flows,
The cunning hunter stealthily goes.
With twinkling eyes and silent tread,
He dances where the wild things spread.

With arrows bright and quiver full,
He whispers tales that hearts can pull.
The forest sings his joyful name,
In this hunter's festive game.

Beneath the stars, the moon aglow,
He tells of creatures, fast and slow.
Each tale a spark, each laugh a cheer,
Echoing loudly, far and near.

So raise a glass to nights of delight,
To the cunning hunter, swift as flight.
In every shadow, every breeze,
His magic wanders, with such ease.

Lurking in the Twilight

In twilight's charm, shadows start to play,
Creatures in waiting, both shy and fey.
Their whispers tickle the cool evening air,
With secrets woven, they dare to share.

The fireflies twinkle, a dance in the night,
Lurking in twilight, they shimmer with light.
A festive spirit encircles the wood,
As laughter and magic in harmony stood.

The leaves weave tales of the daring few,
Who find their joy with each morning dew.
In this realm where day meets the stars,
Adventures bloom, like vibrant, sweet bars.

So gather your friends, let shadows enthrall,
In the twilight's embrace, we summon them all.
Raise a cheer to the mystery, bright and grand,
For in this night, wonders expand.

Camouflage of the Spirit

In vibrant hues, the spirit hides,
Among the flowers, where glee abides.
With a giggle soft and a sway so light,
It blends with nature, sheer delight.

A fluttering dance, a mimic's grace,
Camouflage woven, finds its place.
In jubilant chaos, it twirls and spins,
Where laughter waits, adventure begins.

As shadows lengthen, joy takes flight,
The spirit glows with a festive light.
In every tree, in every call,
It weaves a melody, life's great ball.

So let us join in this wondrous spree,
With the spirit of joy, forever free.
For in nature's heart, we find our cheer,
A festive rhythm that draws us near.

Sly Paths Through the Underbrush

In the thick of trees, where whispers creep,
Sly paths emerge from shadows deep.
Each step a secret, a twist, a turn,
In the festive wild, where passions burn.

With every leaf that rustles low,
The thrill of adventure begins to grow.
Following trails where few have trod,
In the dance of life, we honor the nod.

The underbrush hums with tales untold,
Stories of laughter, brave and bold.
In this maze of wonders, let us delight,
Side by side, through the joyous night.

So gather your courage, your heart, your cheer,
Through sly paths drawn, we hold so dear.
For in this journey, we shall find,
A festive spirit, joy intertwined.

Call of the Cunning

In the glimmer of the night, a whisper sings,
Creatures gather, showcasing their wings,
Glints of mischief dance in their eyes,
A festive night beneath the skies.

Laughter tumbles, echoing clear,
As moonlight drapes the gathering near,
A symphony of sounds fills the air,
In every corner, adventure's flair.

Jests of rabbits and foxes' tricks,
Ancient stories, a playful mix,
With shadows long and spirits bright,
They celebrate beneath the starlight.

So heed the call of cunning friends,
Where every twist and turn transcends,
For in this realm where mischief thrives,
The heart rejoices, and true joy dives.

Twilight Tales of the Forest

As dusk descends, the stories wake,
Whispers flow from every lake,
Twilight air, a dance of glee,
In the forest, wild and free.

Beneath the canopy, shadows play,
Nature hums its soft ballet,
The chorus of crickets adds delight,
To the magic of falling twilight.

Fireflies twinkle, like stars set low,
Painting paths with an enchanting glow,
Branches rustle, secrets shared,
Festive tales, all souls declared.

With every rustle, faint giggles rise,
Mischief weaves, under twilight skies,
Here in the forest, stories inspire,
Hearts ignited, with festive fire.

Voices in the Underbrush

In the thickets, laughter hums,
With every rustle, adventure comes,
Little paws and clever schemes,
Gather 'round under moonlit beams.

Chittering squirrels, tales they weave,
A festive night, they all believe,
Echoing songs of the hidden prize,
With shimmering stars in their eyes.

Misfits of night, both sly and bold,
Share tales of treasures, glimmers of gold,
In every corner, secrets combined,
Voices twirling, hearts entwined.

Through the brush, the festival grows,
A tapestry of life, as the moon glows,
With jubilant cheers, they come alive,
In the underbrush, they forever thrive.

Mirage of the Sly

In the midst of night, where shadows lean,
A mirage appears, a sight serene,
Foxes prance and whispers beckon,
A festive call, a secret reckoned.

Dancing figures, lithe and spry,
Crafting illusions beneath the sky,
With laughter spilling, a joyful chase,
In the mirage, they embrace their space.

Glimmers of mischief weave in the air,
A tapestry spun with utmost care,
Chasing dreams, the sly ones play,
In the night, where wanderers sway.

So join the dance, let the magic rise,
In this mirage, beneath starry skies,
For in their world, every soul is free,
Where festivity blooms, as wild as can be.

Secrets Beneath the Canopy

Beneath the trees, whispers gleam,
Colorful lights in a joyful stream.
Laughter dances on the breeze,
As night wraps the world with glee.

Fireflies twinkle, shadows play,
Friends gather 'round, come what may.
Secrets shared in joyous cheer,
Under the stars, all feels near.

The moon peeks in, casting a glow,
In this sanctuary, our spirits flow.
Every heartbeat sings of delight,
As we celebrate the magical night.

Together we dream, together we laugh,
In the embrace of nature's craft.
For in this moment, we are free,
Secrets bloom beneath the canopy.

Mirage in Moonlight

Under the moon, shadows take flight,
Waltzing softly, the world feels right.
Whispers of secrets with each step traced,
In shimmering light, our fears erased.

Silvered illusions drift through the air,
Crafted by starlight, a magic rare.
We twirl and spin, hearts in a whirl,
As laughter sprinkles, dreams unfurl.

Echoes of joy in the night do sing,
As every moment feels like spring.
Luminous joy, a sweet serenade,
In this mirage, together we're made.

Hand in hand under celestial beams,
We weave together our wildest dreams.
As shadows deepen, let's chase the light,
In this moonlit dance, all feels right.

Harmonies of the Hidden

In the forest, a symphony plays,
Notes of laughter, bright sunrays.
Whispers of joy echo through trees,
With every breeze, a melody frees.

Hidden wonders in colors bloom,
Lifting spirits, dispelling gloom.
Together we sing, hearts intertwined,
In this magical realm, joy we find.

Festive hearts beat, a rhythm divine,
United in spirit, our lives intertwine.
Let the music of laughter bind,
In these moments, true bliss aligned.

As stars awaken, we raise our cheer,
In the quiet, our voices clear.
Harmonies greet the flickering night,
In this gathering, everything feels right.

Jests of the Midnight Traveler

The clock strikes twelve, tales take flight,
A traveler stirs in the soft moonlight.
With a grin wide and heart aglow,
Stories emerge in the midnight show.

Laughter echoes through the trees,
As whimsy dances upon the breeze.
Jests to share, each tale unfolds,
In the arms of night, adventure molds.

Firelight flickers, casting dreams,
Spinning yarns filled with gleams.
Every chuckle, a spark ignites,
In this festival of starry nights.

Let us wander where shadows play,
With a jester's heart, we find our way.
For in these moments, we truly roam,
In laughter's embrace, we find our home.

Shimmers of the Shy Gazelle

In meadows bright, the gazelle leaps,
Her laughter twirls, the soft wind sweeps.
Gold glints dance on a sunlit curve,
Nature's joy, with grace we serve.

Beneath the trees, shadows play,
As petals fall and children sway.
Each shimmer brightens the gentle ground,
In this festivity, pure love is found.

Dewdrops catch the morning light,
In laughter's song, spirits take flight.
Together we join in the vibrant scene,
With shimmers of joy, forever serene.

A festival of colors around us spread,
In the softest breeze, the sweet words are said.
So let us dance, let our hearts engage,
In shimmers of life, we turn the page.

Gleam of the Twilight Trickster

Twilight falls, the sky ignites,
With laughter bright, the heart delights.
The trickster leaps, casting a spell,
In colors rich, all is well.

With shadows long and secrets deep,
The night awakens, it's time to leap.
Magical whispers drift on high,
As stars gather in the velvet sky.

Around the fire, stories spin,
With merry hearts, we all gather in.
A dance of light, a flickering cheer,
In the gleam of twilight, we draw near.

Let mirth abound, let giggles resound,
In joyful chaos, we're blissfully bound.
The trickster plays, oh what a sight,
In joyous gleam of the starry night.

Choreographed by the Moon

The moonlight casts its silver glide,
A dance unfolds, stars as our guide.
With twinkling eyes and hearts in tune,
We're all swept up, choreographed by the moon.

Around the fire, hands entwine,
The night is young, our spirits shine.
Each twirl and leap, a story told,
In the embrace of warmth from the cold.

Whispers of joy, laughter blooms,
As dreams take flight in the starlit rooms.
We move as one, in joyful sway,
Beneath the moon's tender ballet.

In this moment, we are free,
Choreographed with glee, you see.
So let us dance till the break of dawn,
In moonlit magic, forever drawn.

Whispers from the Wile

Through the trees, the whispers roam,
From wile's embrace, we find our home.
With twinkling laughter, secrets weave,
As hearts entwine, we choose to believe.

Underneath the star-spangled night,
Every echo brings pure delight.
In playful winds, the stories flow,
With each gentle breeze, our spirits grow.

Together we gather, hand in hand,
In the shelter of the woodland band.
With whispers soft, we share our dreams,
In every laughter, the joy redeems.

So let the world fade, let time stand still,
In the wile's heart, we dance with will.
With nature's pulse, we sing through the night,
In whispers of love, we find our light.

Prowler's Serenade

In shadows deep, where whispers play,
The moonlight dances, bright and gay.
A melody drifts through the night air,
With notes of joy, a tune so rare.

The stars join in, a twinkling choir,
As laughter swirls, lifting higher.
Footsteps echo on a winding path,
With every turn, a newfound laugh.

Beneath the trees, the revelers sway,
In a wild waltz, they spin and play.
Their spirits lift like balloons on high,
Beneath the moon's soft, watchful eye.

As dawn approaches, joy remains,
A night remembered, free of chains.
With heartbeats quick, they bid farewell,
To the prowler's song, a magic spell.

Woodland Whimsy at Sundown

As light retreats and shadows blend,
The woodland whispers, tales to send.
Frolicsome sprites flit through the trees,
Dancing to the tune of the evening breeze.

Fireflies blink, a soft embrace,
Illuminating the dewy space.
With every flicker, hearts take flight,
A canvas painted in the fading light.

Rustling leaves in playful chatter,
The laughter of elves, a joyful clatter.
Beneath the boughs, the revelers spin,
In this magic realm, where dreams begin.

As night descends, the world aglow,
With whispers of joy from here below.
The woodland holds its breath in cheer,
For every moment, the twilight yearns near.

Dance of the Elusive One

In the clearing bright, where moonlight weaves,
The elusive one twirls, as the forest grieves.
With silken steps, they glide and spin,
A joyful dance where dreams begin.

Echoes of laughter drift through the night,
With every twirl, a spark of light.
Leaves rustle soft, in rhythm and rhyme,
Creating a melody lost in time.

Beneath the stars, a festival bright,
With shadows merging in the silver light.
Catch the moment, an ethereal sight,
As the dance of joy takes off in flight.

And as dawn breaks, the whispers fade,
Leaving a trace of memories made.
In the heart of the woods, the pulse remains,
Of the dance so sweet, in joyful refrains.

Subtle Tones of the Twilight

In twilight's glow, a fragile sigh,
The world transforms, as day waves goodbye.
Soft hues blend in a calming embrace,
Nature celebrates, a tranquil space.

As crickets hum their evening tune,
The stars emerge, one by one, like a boon.
Delight fills the air, a gentle tease,
In this quiet haven, hearts find ease.

Beneath the arches of whispering trees,
Mirthful spirits flicker like a breeze.
With soft laughter, they spin around,
In the depth of dusk, a joy profound.

As night enfolds the world in grace,
Each moment savored, a warm embrace.
With every breath of this twilight glow,
The subtle tones of joy softly flow.

Murmurs of the Moonlit Grove

In the grove where shadows play,
Laughter dances, night is gay.
Leaves are whispering sweet delight,
As the moonbeams fill the night.

Fires twinkle, spirits cheer,
All are welcome, none need fear.
Songs of joy float on the breeze,
In this place of verdant trees.

Cups are raised in festive glee,
Toasting dreams and reverie.
Magic swirls in silver beams,
A tapestry of vibrant dreams.

Together here, we weave our tale,
Under stars that brightly sail.
The night ignites our hearts aglow,
In the grove where friendships grow.

Legends of the Cunning Wanderer

Paths entwine beneath the stars,
The wanderer and tales from afar.
Under the cloak of midnight's charm,
Stories weave, no need for alarm.

With laughter bright, they light the dark,
Each whisper ignites a spark.
Witty quips and clever plays,
Echo through the festive ways.

Through every twist, the fables flow,
Of daring deeds and love's warm glow.
Gathered round, we share and cheer,
As the wanderer's voice draws near.

In this night, adventure's grace,
Unfolds in every smiling face.
Together we weave our own delight,
In the legends of the starlit night.

Flickering Shadows of Enchantment

Candles flicker, shadows play,
Every face in bright array.
Whispers of enchantment soar,
Mysteries linger at the door.

Joyful hearts in circles twine,
With every dance, our spirits shine.
Glowing embers, love's embrace,
In this magical, sacred space.

Moonlight waltzes on the ground,
As we move to a joyful sound.
Spirits rise, the night is young,
In this realm, we all belong.

Let the music fill the air,
Creating magic everywhere.
In the night of festal cheer,
Flickering shadows, bring us near.

Secrets of the Starlit Stalk

In the fields where fireflies blink,
Numbered dreams upon the brink.
Every glow a secret shared,
Underneath the sky so bared.

Together here, we laugh and sigh,
At passing clouds that float on high.
Every moment, pure delight,
Guiding us through velvet night.

The starlit stalk whispers low,
Carrying tales of joy to grow.
Holding memories like a song,
Where we gather, we belong.

With every wish cast to the sky,
In this space, our hopes fly high.
Secrets linger, time stands still,
In the joy of shared goodwill.

Whimsy of the Recurring Trickster

In the twilight's playful glance,
The jester dances, slipping chance.
With mirthful echoes, laughter sings,
Each step a tale, a joy that clings.

Beneath the stars, his shadows play,
Weaving tales till break of day.
With gleeful cheers and mischief bright,
He twirls around, a pure delight.

A flick of wrist, a wink so sly,
He draws a smile from passersby.
In costumes bright, he weaves the night,
With every jest, the world ignites.

So hold your heart, embrace the jest,
Let whimsy guide you; you're the guest.
For in this dance of pure delight,
The trickster laughs, and life feels light.

Glimmers of the Ancient Wanderer

Through woods aglow with firefly light,
An ancient wanderer takes to flight.
His footsteps whisper tales untold,
As gold leaves gather, bold and old.

With every step, the night enthralls,
The echoing laughter, nature calls.
Beneath the moon, his secrets weave,
In dreams of magic, we believe.

Over hills where shadows play,
He shares the dusk, where dreams stray.
With tales of yore, and song anew,
The wanderer's heart is ever true.

So join his dance beneath the trees,
As breezes carry soft-spoken pleas.
For in his steps, the glimmers show,
The ancient paths where wonders flow.

Echoes of Tryst in Thicket

In thickets dense, where secrets dwell,
Two hearts convene; what magic swells!
With whispers soft and glances shy,
They weave a bond beneath the sky.

The rustling leaves, a gentle tune,
As dusk unfurls and greets the moon.
With laughter bright, like stars above,
They trace the lines of budding love.

In hidden nooks where shadows kiss,
The world fades out; they find their bliss.
With stolen moments, time stands still,
In every sigh, a gentle thrill.

So let the thicket hold their dreams,
In echoes soft, where laughter beams.
For in this place of whispered vows,
They find their heart, and love endows.

Veils of Verdant Mystery

In gardens lush, where secrets bloom,
Lies a world wrapped in gentle gloom.
With vines that dance in breezy sighs,
And petals bright that catch the eyes.

Through veils of green, the sunlight spills,
Whispers of magic in the hills.
Each corner turned, a new surprise,
Beneath the watchful, ancient skies.

The flowers nod as breezes play,
Inviting hearts to join the sway.
In every shade, a story spun,
As laughter mingles with the sun.

So wander deep through this expanse,
Where verdant mysteries invite a dance.
For in this garden's warm embrace,
We find ourselves, we find our place.

www.ingramcontent.com/pod-product-compliance
Lightning Source LLC
La Vergne TN
LVHW021306080125
800708LV00005B/915